CHEROKEE

AUG 1 5 1989

DINOSAUR MOUNTAIN
Graveyard of the Past

by CAROLINE ARNOLD

photographs by
RICHARD HEWETT

CLARION BOOKS

NEW YORK

Map on facing page copyright © 1988 by The New York Times Company.
Reprinted by permission.

Photo credits: page 9, National Park Service;
page 10, Carnegie Museum, Pittsburgh, Pennsylvania
Clarion Books
a Houghton Mifflin Company imprint
52 Vanderbilt Avenue, New York, NY 10017
Text copyright © 1989 by Caroline Arnold
Photographs copyright © 1989 by Richard Hewett

Library of Congress Cataloging-in-Publication Data

Arnold, Caroline.
Dinosaur mountain: graveyard of the past / by Caroline Arnold; photographs by Richard Hewett.
p.   cm.
Includes index.
Summary: Describes the work of paleontologists in learning about
dinosaurs, especially the discoveries made at Dinosaur National
Monument in Utah.
ISBN 0-89919-693-4
1. Dinosaurs—Juvenile literature.   2. Dinosaur National Monument
(Colo. and Utah)—Juvenile literature.   3. Paleontology—Juvenile
literature.   [1. Dinosaurs.   2. Dinosaur National Monument
(Colo. and Utah)   3. Paleontology.]   I. Hewett, Richard, ill.   II. Title.
QE862.D5A75   1989   567.9'1'0979221—dc19   88-30218
                                                                        CIP
                                                                        AC

Y 10 9 8 7 6 5 4 3 2 1

ACKNOWLEDGMENTS

We are grateful to the park rangers and staff of the Dinosaur National Monument quarry visitor center, Jensen, Utah, for their cheerful cooperation and assistance with this project. In particular, we thank Dan Chure, Park Paleontologist, and Ann Schaffer, Museum Technician, for their expert advice and for providing us with information about the quarry and the fossils in it. We also thank Cindy George of the Dinosaur Valley Museum of Western Colorado in Grand Junction, Colorado; Alden H. Hamblin of the Utah Field House Natural History State Park in Vernal, Utah; the Carnegie Museum, Pittsburgh, Pennsylvania; the Los Angeles County Museum of Natural History; and the National Park Service for their assistance with the photographs.

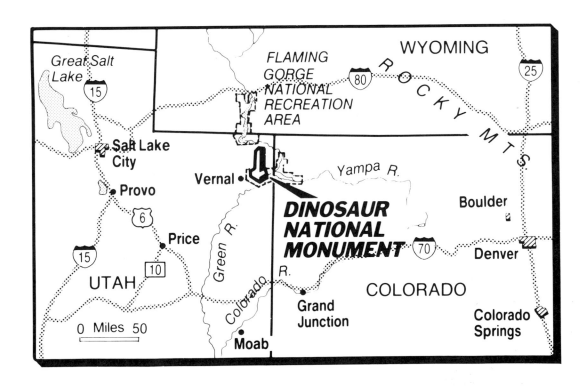

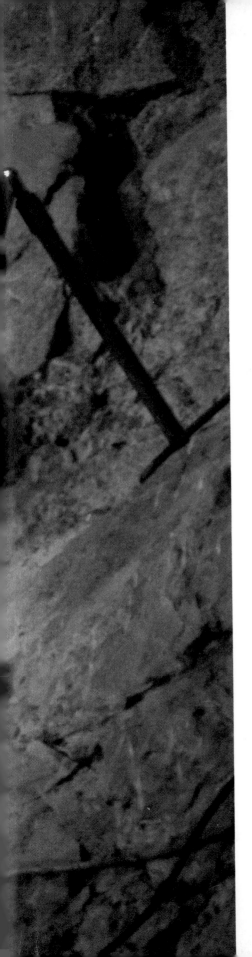

High on a mountain ridge in eastern Utah, a scientist chisels into a sandstone cliff. As small pieces of rock fall away, an enormous fossilized bone slowly emerges. Embedded in the rock nearby are other huge bones, some of them as large as a person. These ancient bones once belonged to giant reptiles called dinosaurs, the largest animals ever to live on earth. What we know about dinosaurs today we have learned from studying fossils such as these at Dinosaur National Monument in Utah.

People who study fossils are called paleontologists, and they look for clues to what life might have been like long ago. A fossil is any trace or remains of ancient life. It may be part of a plant or animal that has been preserved unchanged, or one whose structure has been replaced with minerals. A fossil may also be made when a plant or animal makes an impression, or imprint, in mud or fine sand that later becomes preserved as stone. Both fossil bones and impressions have been found at Dinosaur National Monument.

The age of dinosaurs lasted from about 230 million to approximately 60 million years ago. The fossil bones found at Dinosaur National Monument came from animals that lived in the middle of the dinosaur age, about 145 million years ago. At that time, the high plateaus, deep canyons, and rocky mountains of western North America had not yet been formed. Instead, the land was flat, crisscrossed by winding rivers.

Many kinds of dinosaurs inhabited this ancient landscape. When they died, their bodies decayed and most of their bones disappeared. However, a few animals died on or near an ancient riverbank. When the river flooded, their bodies were washed downstream, and some of them stuck in a sandbar. As the dead bodies lodged in the sand, many were broken apart by the river current or by animals that came to eat them. The loose bones scattered and piled up in heaps, creating a giant bone jigsaw puzzle.

(Left) The Green River winds its way through the mountains of Dinosaur National Monument.

(Right) A model of a *Camarasaurus* appears to search for food among the treetops.

Slowly, the sandbar and its bones were covered with more sand, dirt, and rocks. Eventually, the sand hardened and became sandstone rock. Over millions of years, many more layers of rock formed on top of the dinosaur bones. Then, toward the end of the dinosaur age, the earth in western North America began to rise and form ridges and mountains. In some places, old rock layers that had been deep within the earth were raised to the surface again.

In 1908, Earl Douglass, a paleontologist from the Carnegie Museum in Pittsburgh, Pennsylvania, began to search the cliff faces and mountain ridges of eastern Utah for traces of dinosaurs. He knew that fossilized bones had been found in similar places nearby in Colorado and Wyoming. Throughout this region, there is a layer of sandstone rock called the Morrison Formation. A formation is a series of rock layers that all have the same characteristics. The Morrison Formation was created between 145 and 135 million years ago and is a rich source of dinosaur fossils from a time of the earth's history called the Jurassic period.

(Left) Rocks in the Morrison Formation often appear as rounded, multicolored ridges.

(Right) Earl Douglass.

On August 17, 1909, Douglass climbed to the top of a rocky ridge where wind and rain had washed away much of the dirt, revealing layers of older rock underneath. He looked down and saw below him a neatly arranged row of dinosaur tailbones. They belonged to the dinosaur called *Apatosaurus* (ah-PAT-uh-SOR-us), more commonly known as *Brontosaurus* (BRON-tuh-SOR-us).

This discovery marked the beginning of one of the most spectacular dinosaur finds of this century. Further digging revealed these bones to be the most complete *Apatosaurus* skeleton ever discovered. In addition, the fossil quarry contained thousands of other bones belonging to at least sixty other dinosaurs.

Ten different kinds of dinosaurs have been identified from the fossils found at the quarry. They include more than half of all the known types of dinosaurs that lived in North America during the late Jurassic period.

The bones removed from the quarry by Douglass and his crew were taken to the Carnegie Museum. There they were catalogued, and some were assembled into skeletons and put on display. Later, fossil bones were also collected at the Utah quarry for the Smithsonian Institution in Washington, D.C., and the University of Utah in Salt Lake City. Over a period of fifteen years, thousands of fossils weighing a total of more than 700,000 pounds (315,000 kilograms) were removed from the site.

Most assembled skeletons exhibited in museums are made of bones from several animals because complete skeletons are rarely found. In cases where bones are missing, artificial ones are sometimes used to make the skeleton look complete. Comparisons with other dinosaur fossils and with modern reptile skeletons help scientists figure out the shape and size of missing bones.

Dinosaur Hall at the Carnegie Museum, Pittsburgh. Skeletons from left to right: *Allosaurus*, *Diplodocus*, *Tyrannosaurus rex*, *Apatosaurus*, and *Stegosaurus*.

Like most fossil skeletons, Douglass's *Apatosaurus* skeleton had been found without a head. Fossil heads of dinosaurs are rarer than other kinds of bones because the more fragile bones of the skull are easily crushed or lost. Although the workmen at the quarry found a head nearby that fit onto the *Apatosaurus* neck bones, it could not be said for certain that it was the head belonging to that animal.

Scientists debated for several years what kind of head should be placed on the *Apatosaurus* skeleton displayed in the Carnegie Museum. Finally, they decided to use a *Camarasaurus* (KAM-uh-ruh-SOR-us) head from the museum collection. This turned out to be a famous dinosaur mistake. It was not until 1979 that it was replaced with a replica of the actual head. The correct head was the one found near the skeleton in the quarry; it is the only known *Apatosaurus* skull.

The dinosaur quarry discovered by Earl Douglass is one of the most valuable sources of fossils ever found. It has more complete or nearly complete dinosaur skeletons, more well-preserved dinosaur skulls, and more skeletons of young dinosaurs than any other site.

In 1915, the United States government declared the quarry and eighty acres of the surrounding land to be a national monument. However, after 1923, when Douglass stopped working there, little was done to develop the park, even though many bones remained. Finally, in 1958, a visitor center was constructed at the quarry site and excavation was resumed. The building, called the Dinosaur Quarry, is now a museum and a place where visitors can view dinosaur bones and watch paleontologists at work.

Rear view of the Dinosaur Quarry; the sloping cliff face forms the left wall of the building.

(Right) Park rangers help visitors learn more about dinosaurs discovered in the quarry.

(Below) This *Apatosaurus* leg bone, partially embedded in the quarry wall, is over 4 feet (1.2 meters) long.

An unusual feature of the Dinosaur Quarry is that part of the quarry itself forms the rear wall of the building. This portion of the wall, which is about one-third of the original quarry, contains more than 2,000 bones.

When the Dinosaur Quarry was built, it was decided that the

bottom layer of fossils would be left partially exposed in the rock face. Thus, visitors could see exactly how the bones had been deposited. Only when excavation on the wall shows that a bone is covering one underneath is the top bone removed. It will take about fifteen more years to reveal all the bones remaining in the wall.

Paleontologists measure and compare fossil bones to learn what dinosaurs may have looked like, what they ate, and how they behaved.

Paleontologists identify fossil bones by comparing them with similar bones found at other locations. Each time a scientist discovers a fossil bone that seems to belong to a new animal, that dinosaur is given a name. Most of the scientific names of dinosaurs are derived from Latin or Greek words, which often reflect what scientists thought the animals must have been like. The word *dinosaur* comes from two Greek words meaning "terrible lizard."

Sometimes the bones of the same species of dinosaur have been found in two different places, and the animal was given two different names. This is what happened to one of the most well-known of all dinosaurs, *Apatosaurus*, or *Brontosaurus*. When the bones of this dinosaur were first discovered, the animal was named *Apatosaurus*, meaning "deceptive lizard," because of its unbelievable size. A few years later, the same scientist found other large bones at another site and thought they belonged to a new dinosaur. He named this dinosaur *Brontosaurus*, meaning "thunder lizard," because he thought that the animal was so big it must have made a noise like thunder when it walked. Only later did other scientists realize that both sets of bones belonged to the same kind of dinosaur.

It is customary to use the name first given to an animal as the correct one. Thus, *Apatosaurus* is the correct scientific name for this dinosaur, even though many people still call it *Brontosaurus*.

Collections of fossil bones help scientists to identify new discoveries.

Scientists divide the different kinds of dinosaurs into two large groups according to their body shapes. One group, the saurischians (sawr-ISS-kee-uns), whose name means "lizard hips," has hips shaped more like those of modern lizards. The other group, ornithischians (ore-nith-ISS-kee-uns), whose name means "bird hips," has hip-bones shaped like those of birds. About three-quarters of the bones found at the Dinosaur National Monument quarry are from a large group of saurischians called sauropods (SAWR-uh-pods), which means "lizard feet." Sauropods lived for a period of 147 million years, reaching their height in the late Jurassic period.

The sauropods include all the largest dinosaurs that ever walked the earth. They were gigantic, long-necked, long-tailed creatures. All of these animals developed strong, sturdy leg bones to help support their enormous weight.

At one time, scientists thought that sauropods must have spent much of their time in water, where it would have been easier to move their heavy bodies. Now they believe that sauropods lived mostly on land. There they used their long necks to eat leaves from the tops of trees, in much the same way that modern giraffes do.

Diplodocus model peers out from the trees in the Dinosaur Garden at the Utah Field House of Natural History in Vernal, Utah.

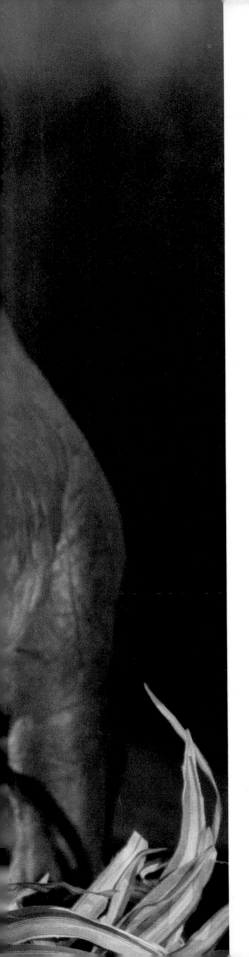

The bones of sauropods found in the quarry include those of *Apatosaurus*, *Barosaurus* (BARE-uh-SOR-us), *Camarasaurus*, and *Diplodocus* (dih-PLOD-uh-kus). Of these, *Apatosaurus* is the largest. The skeleton excavated by Douglass in 1909 measures 76½ feet (23 meters) long and is 14 feet 8 inches (4.5 meters) high at the hips. The living animal is estimated to have weighed up to 35 tons (32,000 kilograms). Other fossils indicate that some *Apatosaurus* may have grown even bigger, up to 90 feet (28 meters) long! These huge animals must have had enormous appetites. It is estimated that an adult *Apatosaurus* ate 1¾ tons (1,600 kilograms) of food each day.

Recent discoveries of *Apatosaurus* footprints suggest that these dinosaurs lived in herds. Footprints of different sizes indicate the herd included both young and old animals. It is likely that adults looked after the young dinosaurs as they were growing up.

Bones of a sauropod similar to *Apatosaurus*, but not as heavy, have also been found at the quarry. That dinosaur has been named *Barosaurus* from a Greek word meaning "weight" because of the very large bones in its neck.

Model of a mother *Apatosaurus* and her baby on display at the Dinosaur Valley Museum in Grand Junction, Colorado.

A cast of the juvenile *Camarasaurus* skeleton, positioned almost as it was when it was discovered, is being prepared for display at the Dinosaur Quarry. (The original skeleton is at the Carnegie Museum in Pittsburgh.)

An adult *Camarasaurus* skull, still attached to the spinal column, is one of two exposed skulls in the quarry wall. Large nostril openings are visible just below the eyeholes.

The sauropod most commonly found in the Morrison Formation is called *Camarasaurus*. Its name refers to the hollow chambers in its backbone. Many *Camarasaurus* bones are often found together, indicating that these dinosaurs also probably lived in groups. The *Camarasaurus* was somewhat more stocky than *Apatosaurus*. Two species of *Camarasaurus* have been found. The larger species, *Camarasaurus supremus*, grew to be 60 feet (19 meters) long and weighed 32 tons (28,000 kilograms). *Camarasaurus lentus* was somewhat smaller at 35 feet (12 meters) and 16 tons (14,000 kilograms.)

Most skeletons are found with many bones missing, so when Douglass found a nearly complete skeleton of a young *Camarasaurus lentus*, it was a remarkable discovery. This is one of the most complete dinosaur skeletons ever found.

Another sauropod found in the quarry wall is *Diplodocus*, the longest dinosaur known. Its skeleton measures 84 feet (26 meters) from end to end. The name *Diplodocus* means "double beam" and refers to the T-shaped bones in its tail. *Diplodocus* may have used its extremely long tail as a whip to defend itself against predators.

Although *Diplodocus* was very long, it did not weigh nearly as much as *Apatosaurus* because it was much more slender. Scientists estimate that the weight of an adult *Diplodocus* was about 12 tons (11,000 kilograms).

In the front of its mouth, *Diplodocus* had a row of peg-shaped teeth. The teeth would not have been very useful for chewing, but some scientists think they may have been used to pluck leaves from the branches of tall trees.

In some places, scientists have found small, polished stones, called gastroliths, near dinosaur skeletons. The stones suggest that dinosaurs may have had digestive systems something like those of modern birds. Like birds, which eat gravel with their food, the dinosaurs ate the pebbles. After food was swallowed, it would mix with the stones and break into smaller, more easily digested pieces.

(Above) The teeth of *Diplodocus*, seen here in a mirror, grew at a forward angle in the front of its mouth.

(Right) Gastroliths are small, polished stones that may have helped a dinosaur digest food.

(Facing page) This cast of a *Diplodocus* skeleton stands in the Dinosaur Garden at the Utah Field House in Vernal, Utah.

Theropods (THAIR-uh-pods) are the other group of saurischians. Unlike the sauropods, which were all plant-eating animals, the theropods were meat eaters and ate other dinosaurs. Just as in the present-day world, in which there are fewer meat eaters than plant eaters, so it was in Jurassic times. Fossils of theropods are not as commonly found as those of sauropods.

Also found in the quarry was the largest and fiercest enemy of the plant-eaters, the meat-eating *Allosaurus* (AL-uh-SOR-us). *Allosaurus*, whose name means "other lizard," is sometimes also called *Antrodemus* (an-troh-DEE-mus). An adult *Allosaurus* was 30 to 35 feet (9–11 meters) long and weighed 1 to 2½ tons (900–2,200 kilograms). It walked only on its hind legs and used its long tail to balance the weight of its heavy neck and head. Its shorter forelimbs were armed with sharp claws that were used to grasp and tear its prey.

Sometimes museums make casts, or copies, of dinosaur skeletons for display. This cast of an *Allosaurus* skeleton is at the Dinosaur Valley Museum in Grand Junction, Colorado.

Although *Allosaurus* was big, it was not nearly as big as some of the sauropods that were its prey. It probably ate dinosaurs that were weakened or young and small. It also may have been a scavenger, feeding upon dinosaurs that were already dead. Because *Allosaurus* fossils are sometimes found in groups, scientists think that they may have hunted in packs as modern wolves do.

The huge jaws of *Allosaurus* were lined with sharp, jagged teeth, ideal for tearing apart chunks of meat. Like the jaws of modern snakes and lizards, those of *Allosaurus* were flexible and could open wide to allow *Allosaurus* to swallow pieces of food larger than its normal mouth size.

(Left) An *Allosaurus* model appears to be searching for prey along a riverbank.

(Below) Two *Allosaurus* skeletons, including a nearly perfect skull, have been found at the Dinosaur Quarry. The large openings in the skull help reduce its weight, making it easier for the neck to support the head.

(Above) Tooth and jawbone of *Ceratosaurus*.

(Facing page) Concrete model of *Ceratosaurus* in front of the Utah Field House in Vernal, Utah.

Another predator whose fossil bones are found at the Dinosaur Quarry is *Ceratosaurus* (sair-AT-uh-SOR-us). This dinosaur, whose name means "horned lizard," was about 18 feet (5.5 meters) long and weighed 1 to 1½ tons (900–1,400 kilograms). Slightly smaller than *Allosaurus*, *Ceratosaurus* is distinguished by a horn on its snout.

A few bones of a third, much smaller, predator have also been found at the quarry. There is not enough evidence to be sure to what animal they belong, but they probably are from a dinosaur called *Ornitholestes* (ore-nith-uh-LESS-teez), which means "bird robber." Its discoverer gave it this name because he thought that its agile shape allowed it to snatch birds out of the air. *Ornitholestes* stood about 6 to 10 feet (1.8–3.2 meters) tall and weighed 200 to 300 pounds (90–135 kilograms).

The ornithischian, or bird-hipped, dinosaurs are represented at the Dinosaur Quarry by three kinds of dinosaurs — *Stegosaurus* (steg-uh-SOR-us), *Dryosaurus* (DRY-uh-SOR-us), and *Campto-saurus* (KAMP-tuh-SOR-us).

Stegosaurus, whose name means "plated lizard," is one of the strangest-looking dinosaurs of all. Its head, which was about 18 inches (0.5 meter) long, contained a tiny brain the size of a walnut, its tail ended in long spikes, and its back was lined with a double row of large, flat plates. This slow-moving, plant-eating dinosaur was about 20 to 25 feet (6–8 meters) long and weighed 2 to 5 tons (1,800–4,600 kilograms).

No one knows what color dinosaurs might have been. Perhaps they were brightly hued, as is this *Stegosaurus* model displayed at the Dinosaur Valley Museum in Grand Junction, Colorado.

Perhaps the most unusual and mysterious feature of *Stegosaurus* was the row of vertical plates along its back. Scientists have developed several theories regarding their use. The plates may have been for protection, or they might have been used to impress other stegosaurs. They might have helped to regulate body temperature. Possibly they served all three purposes.

Following the sauropods, *Stegosaurus* is the next most commonly found fossil in the quarry. Large, flat *Stegosaurus* plates can be seen in several places on the quarry wall. Not many bones of young stegosaurs have ever been found, so the partial skeleton of a small *Stegosaurus* that was discovered there is unusual.

The double row of triangular plates along its spine is a unique feature of *Stegosaurus.*

(Above) Unlike many dinosaurs, *Camptosaurus* could grasp objects with five long fingers on its front feet.

(Left) Cast of *Camptosaurus* skeleton.

Dryosaurus and *Camptosaurus* both belong to a group of ornithischians called ornithopods (ORE-nith-uh-pods), meaning "bird feet." Bones of these plant-eating dinosaurs are relatively rare in the Dinosaur Quarry.

By dinosaur standards, *Dryosaurus* was quite small, measuring only 9 feet (2.7 meters) in length and standing about 6 feet (1.8 meters) tall. It could run quickly on its long legs and could probably easily escape predators such as *Allosaurus*. The name *Dryosaurus* means "oak lizard."

Camptosaurus was a somewhat larger relative of *Dryosaurus*. There were several species of *Camptosaurus*, ranging in size from 6 to 20 feet (1.8–6 meters) in length and 900 to 1,500 pounds (400–700 kilograms) in weight. The name *Camptosaurus* means "bent lizard," referring to the shape of its hip bone. Members of the *Camptosaurus* family are the ancestors of the more recent duck-billed dinosaurs, or hadrosaurs (HAD-ruh-sors), that lived from 140 to 65 million years ago.

Dinosaurs were not the only animals trapped in the ancient sandbar. At the Dinosaur Quarry, the most common fossils are those of freshwater clams. Ancient crocodiles and turtles also inhabited the river valley. Unlike the dinosaurs, their descendants lived on to the present day.

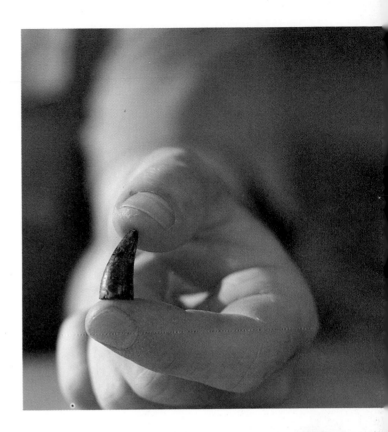

(Above) This fossil crocodile tooth belonged to a now-extinct species called *Goniopholis* (GAH-ni-uh-FO-lis.)

(Right) This ancient turtle shell is almost perfectly preserved.

An *Apatosaurus* backbone slowly
emerges from a rocky hillside.

As paleontologists explore the mountains and ridges of western North America, more and more evidence of life in the Jurassic age is discovered. Within Dinosaur National Monument alone, more than one hundred sites containing dinosaur fossils have been located. Most of these sites have been left to be excavated in the future unless it is necessary to protect the fossils from weather damage.

At some sites within the park, scientists have found the remains of smaller animals that lived at the same time as dinosaurs. The animals include early mammals and some smaller dinosaurs. By identifying the wildlife and plants that might have provided food and shelter for dinosaurs, scientists can develop a more complete picture of what life might have been like millions of years ago.

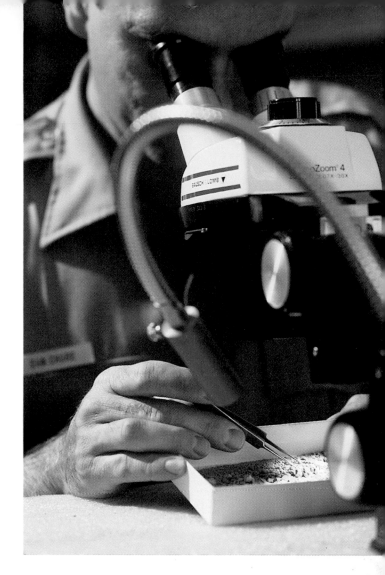

(Above) Some fossils are so small that they must be studied under a microscope.

(Right) This tiny tooth belonged to a small dinosaur about the size of a modern turkey.

(Above) Dinosaur eggshells. (Below) Ultrasaurus shoulder bone.

New information about dinosaurs is being found all over the world. Discoveries of fossilized dinosaur eggs and young animals reveal more about the growth and development of these huge reptiles. Fossil footprints provide clues to the daily activities of dinosaurs.

In recent years, scientists in Utah and Colorado have uncovered bones of animals they think may be the biggest dinosaurs of all. These supergiants may have stood over 60 feet (19 meters) tall and weighed more than 100 tons (88,000 kilograms)! Scientists do not yet know if these are new kinds of dinosaurs or just very large individuals of already known kinds. Until they find out, the new dinosaurs have been nicknamed supersaurus and ultrasaurus for their enormous size.

New discoveries have caused scientists to change their minds about what dinosaurs were like. We used to think that dinosaurs were stupid, slow-moving animals found mainly in swamps. Now we believe that they were well adapted to their environment, they may have had complex social lives, and they probably lived on dry land. Dinosaurs were a highly successful animal that lasted for 170 million years. In contrast, people have lived on earth for only half a million years.

Many theories have been developed to explain why dinosaurs became extinct. Maybe the climate changed so that it was too hot or too cold for dinosaurs. Possibly the plants changed so much that dinosaurs could not find enough food. Or perhaps a giant asteroid from outer space crashed into the earth and created a layer of dust that blocked the sunlight. Without the sun it would have been cold, the plants would have died, and the animals would not have had enough to eat. A new theory suggests that the amount of oxygen in the earth's atmosphere changed about the same time dinosaurs became extinct, and that may be what killed them.

Fossils like those found in the quarry at Dinosaur National Monument provide clues to what life was like 145 million years ago or more. We may never know exactly why dinosaurs disappeared. Yet, as we learn more about life in dinosaur times, we will learn how the earth changed in the past and understand better the planet we live on today.

Stegosaurus model outside the Dinosaur Quarry visitor center.

INDEX

Page numbers in *italics* refer to illustrations.

ABOUT THE AUTHOR

Caroline Arnold says that until she began working on *Dinosaur Mountain*, her experience with dinosaurs had been limited to viewing fossils in museum exhibits. But at Dinosaur National Monument in Utah, she camped beside the Green River and walked through an area rich in fossils. "Although the landscape has changed much in 145 million years, it was still easy for me to imagine dinosaurs gathering at a similar river long ago. Suddenly, those giant animals seemed very real to me."

Caroline Arnold lives in Los Angeles, California, and teaches writing for children at UCLA Extension. She has written four other books for Clarion: *Pets Without Homes*, *Music Lessons for Alex*, *Trapped in Tar*, and *Juggler*.

ABOUT THE PHOTOGRAPHER

Richard Hewett found photographing the quarry wall at Dinosaur National Monument to be a special challenge. If photographed during the day, the fossil bones in the wall were practically invisible on film. The color of the bones blended too well with the surrounding rock. In order to get the dramatic pictures he wanted, Mr. Hewett had to photograph the wall at night using special high-power lighting equipment.

Richard Hewett, who also lives in Los Angeles, is a fulltime freelance photographer. Besides taking photographs for Caroline Arnold's books, Mr. Hewett has collaborated with his wife, Joan, on several other books for Clarion. They include *Motorcycle on Patrol* and *On Camera: The Story of a Child Actor*.